Osoto-Gari

JUDO MASTERCLASS TECHNIQUES

OSOTO-GARI

Yasuhiro Yamashita

First published in 1991 by
The Crowood Press
Ramsbury, Marlborough,
Wiltshire SN8 2HE

This edition published in 1992 by
Fighting FIlms Ltd
PO Box 2405
Bristol
BS1 9BA
Telephone: +44 (0)845 408 5836
Fax: +44 (0)117 929 4540
www.fightingfilms.com
E-mail: info@fightingfilms.com

Reprinted 1997, 2001, 2008

British Library Cataloguing in Publication Data
 Yamashita, Yasuhiro
 Osoto-gari : judo masterclass techniques
 1. Judo
 1. Title
 796.8152

ISBN 978 0 9518455 8 5

Acknowledgments
Many people contributed to this book. First of all, my thanks
must go to my teacher, Nobuyuki Sato, who offered valuable
advice both at a technical and a historical level. Secondly, my
students at Tokai University proved tireless in their role as uke
despite the arduous photo sessions. My thanks must also go to
Yoshinori Nagase of Kindai Judo, always so willing to help with
photographic material. The bulk of the competition
photographs came from the seemingly limitless portfolio of the
leading European specialist judo photographer, David Finch.
Both the words and photographs for the self-defence section
came from Edward Ferrie, 3rd Dan, who is so eminently
equipped to write about the subject. To all these, and others, I
offer my thanks.

Typeset by Acuté, Stroud, Glos.
Printed in Great Britain by 4word Ltd, Bristol

Contents

Foreword

Osoto-gari has always been one of the most popular of judo throws in spite of its general classification as a technique used most frequently by middleweights and above. Despite its apparently simple mechanical principles, it is a throw as complex in its nuances and as rich in its variations as any of the other major throws.

There could be no better guide to *osoto-gari* than Yasuhiro Yamashita. Ever since he burst on to the international scene as a teenager in 1976, he dominated judo in a way that few would have thought possible with the growing international status of the sport. From that unforgettable day in the Tournoi de Paris until he retired, in 1985, he was unbeaten, winning a record nine All-Japan Championships, the Olympic Open title in 1984 and world titles in 1979, 1981 and 1983. As a competitor, his judo was underpinned by an intense determination to do his best. This was not merely a question of raw ambition but a deep-rooted vision of what a human being is capable of when faced with Mount Everest in the shape of a massive Russian opponent, Sergei Novikov, or his much larger Japanese rival, Hitoshi Saito. Yamishita never lost.

What was even more notable was that, throughout, his judo technique was distinguished by a high level of competence in both *tachiwaza* and *newaza*, backed by perfect preparation. Whatever his heart felt — after all, judo is not an activity for the chicken-hearted — Yamashita always maintained a courteous and considerate presence.

During his competitive career, he developed a particular understanding for a number of throws, including *uchimata* and *ouchi-gari*, but his *osoto-gari* always remained his *tokui-*

(a) Here, in the 1983 All-Japan Championships, I have dashed into an osoto-gari *but my opponent, Fujiwara, has managed to twist away. This is where the attacking leg must continue to reap strongly, and not just hook passively. This is a very common position in competition and the success of the throw depends largely on the attacking leg never letting up.*

waza (favourite technique). When invited to contribute to this series, he showed no hesitation in chosing *osoto-gari*.

Though he specialised in a particularly dynamic form of *osoto-gari*, he has made a continuing study of other variations. This book is the fruit of that study. It represents Yamashita's viewpoint, and a view of Japanese judo at its peak. In so doing it is an outstanding contribution to the *Masterclass* series.

Nicolas Soames
Masterclass
Series Editor

Michi or Do – Road or Way

Osoto-Gari: A Personal View

Osoto-gari was the first technique I learned at my junior high school, Toen, in Kyushu. It was the strongest high school in Japan (for a nine-year period its top team was undefeated). I joined when I was twelve because I had shown promise after just two years of judo.

During my elementary school days I had used a range of techniques – *ouchi-gari*, *tai-otoshi* and maybe even *osoto-gari* occasionally – but always executed on the right. However, my new teacher at Toen, Reisuke Shiraishi, said that if I wanted to become a world champion, I would have to change to left *kumite* (left grip) because opponents would find it more difficult. The first throw he taught me was *osoto-gari*. There were various reasons for this, though he was probably principally influenced by my size. Although I was only twelve, I was already 90kg and 175cm tall, just five centimetres short of my adult height. I was the heaviest and tallest in the school even though I was only in the first year. Osoto-gari seemed an obvious choice.

Shiraishi-Sensei was far-sighted not only

because he changed my grip from right to left, but also in the way he taught me *osoto-gari*. It would have been easy for him to let me take the high collar grip – after all, I had the height to do it – but he insisted that I take the lapel grip, which is more difficult. 'When you are older, you will probably fight many people in Japan who are lighter and smaller, but abroad you will fight much bigger men', I remember him telling me. 'So you must master middle-weight judo. You must learn to throw your opponents with technique and skill, not just using your weight or power.'

For three or four months, I practised only *osoto-gari*. He insisted that I concentrate on breaking the balance rather than just powering my way through. Then I had to do extra *uchikomi*, working almost immediately on moving *uchikomi*. Timing, said Shiraishi-Sensei, was crucial.

I thought that it would take me a year or two, not only to learn the new throw, but also to become comfortable with the left grip, but I did not really feel awkward with it at all. After a month, I felt quite comfortable. I had joined Toen in May and in July, a month after my thirteenth birthday, I went into a Dan grading and won all my three fights. I used *osoto-gari* in each one. In the first fight, I threw *osoto-gari* for ippon. In the second, *osoto-gari* for *waza-ari* and then I went straight into *osae-komi*. The third fight, I won with two *waza-aris*, both from *osoto-gari*.

Shiraishi-Sensei revealed the plan he had prepared for me. First of all, I would learn *osoto-gari*, then *ouchi-gari*, because they made a useful pair for combination work. To these two I would add *sasae-tsuri-komi-ashi*, which again worked well with *osoto-gari*, and finally, *uchimata*.

While I gradually added these techniques to my repertoire, he instructed me never to use *harai-goshi*, because this was a technique largely for tall men on smaller men and he said I would not meet very many smaller men abroad. I do not know how he knew that I

would fight at international level because you can never really tell with a thirteen-year-old, no matter how successful he may be at that age. I think he just had a strong intuition, but it was his teaching that made my body and my judo. I felt we had a particularly close relation-ship – he only needed to say one thing and I understood three or four.

While I was in my second year, I felt that I had mastered the moving *uchikomi* practice of *osoto-gari*, and started working on *ouchi-gari* and *sasae-tsuri-komi-ashi*. It was just after my fourteenth birthday, when I was still in the second year, that I was able to confirm my progress with my first big competition, the All-Japan Junior High School Team Competi-tion. I was the first boy out for my team and during the day I won all my six fights, throwing five opponents with *osoto-gari* for ippon and one *osoto-gari* for *waza-ari* followed up by *osaekomi* for ippon. My team won the event.

My technical range broadened at senior-high-school level, and settled while I was at Tokai University. I came to realise that apart from being the first major throwing technique that I had learned, *osoto-gari* was becoming very much the central technique in my reper-toire. But it was not a question of steady, uninterrupted progress. In randori during my school and university days, I attacked again and again with it. Sometimes I was countered, but this made me all the more determined to throw that particular opponent with it. I did not switch to another technique to gain my revenge, but went straight back into the attack with *osoto-gari*, just making sure that I broke my opponent's balance more carefully or improved my timing.

When I was in my third year at senior high school (at seventeen) I fought in the All-Japan Championships for the first time. In the quarter-finals I met Hirowake Ishikawa, the captain of Chuo University. It was boy against man, but all the concentrated *osoto-gari* practice paid off and I threw him with *osoto-gari* for ippon. However, I was not yet strong enough to contain Haruki Uemura, who had won the All-Japan Championships the previous year, and he threw me for yuko, to my chagrin, using *osoto-gari*! He went on to win the title for the second year running.

The following year, I had my first experience of judo competition in the West. I travelled with the Japanese squad to the Tournoi de Paris in January 1976 and won it, beating the Russian Givki Onashvili in the final. He retired directly afterwards. This Tournoi de Paris was not without a memorable incident in the earlier rounds. I had thrown Jean-Pierre Tripet (France) with *osoto-gari* for waza-ari and then held Adler, the tall Dutchman, before meeting Wallace of Australia. I went ahead with a koka from *ouchi-gari* and then attacked with *osoto-gari*. I felt that it was not going to work and I started to come out, but Wallace, timing his move to perfection, swept me off my feet with *okuri-ashi-barai*. The referee called ippon, the judges downgraded it to *waza-ari* and I managed to retrieve the match with *osaekomi*. It was a close-run thing though, and it taught me a little more about *osoto-gari* — to be vigilant even when the technique fails.

Although I did not go to the Montreal Olympics, I will never forget watching the heavyweight final between Sergey Novikov (Soviet Union) and Gunther Neureuter (West Germany). Novikov threw Neureuter with a huge *osoto-gari* that confirmed my love for the throw. It was not a particularly beautiful technique but it was packed with Russian power. I remember thinking that if Neureuter had not been a judo man, accustomed to being thrown, he would have died.

The following year I won my first All-Japan Championships, at the age of nineteen, and *osoto-gari* won me the first and fourth rounds. In 1978, I won it again in an even more encouraging manner. Chonuske Takagi had won the heavyweight category in the 1973 World Championships so he was a highly experienced fighter. He was also an *osoto-gari* specialist and, in an extremely hard-

fought battle in the final, I threw him with *osoto-gari* for ippon.

For the next seven years, until my retirement from competition, in 1985, *osoto-gari* continued to win me many matches. In the frequent meetings with Jean-Luc Rouge (France), one of my strongest foreign opponents, I used *osoto-gari* often, with success, most memorably throwing him for *waza-ari* and then again for yuko in the final of the 1979 World Championships in Paris.

My best *osoto-gari* came, I think, in the semi-finals of the All-Japan Championships in 1983, when I threw Takao Fujiwara. While I had been working on my *osoto-gari* over the years, I had in my mind an ideal throw in which the entry and the *kuzushi* and the throw were perfect. I had scored many ippons by 1983, but I had not attained that ideal standard.

Looking back over the whole of my career, that throw on Fujiwara was the best, being both dynamic to feel and beautiful to see.

Uemura was not the only man to throw me with *osoto-gari* in contest. When I was in my second year of high school, Kazuhiro Ninomiya, one of the great *osoto-gari* specialists of the 1970s (he was Olympic Champion in 1972), threw me with it, and in my penultimate year of competition, at the Los Angeles Olympics, Laurent del Colombo (France) scored a *koka*. I had injured my right leg in the first round and when Del Colombo attacked it using his long legs I turned my body away from the throw, but realised only too late that I was not able to pull my leg out of his reach in time. It gave me a bit of a shock, but fortunately, I was able to throw him with *ouchi-gari* and then hold him with *yoko-shiho-gatame*.

Although *osoto-gari* is my *tokui-waza*, it has not been my most successful technique in competition. Of the contests I won with *tachi-waza*, around 35 per cent came from my *uchimata*, followed by 30 per cent from *osoto-gari*, with *ouchi-gari* and other miscellaneous techniques completing the total.

This is contrasted by my randori practice,

(a) and (b) In the Seoul Olympic Games, as Peter Seisenbacher was heading for his historic second middleweight title, he encountered Kim (Korea) and dispatched him with osoto-gari *for ippon.*

where I have used *osoto-gari* around 40 per cent of the time, with *uchimata* around 30 per cent, followed by *ouchi-gari* and *sasae-tsuri-komi-ashi*. Part of the reason for this is that in contest (especially as the years went by) my opponents became increasingly reluctant to attack me. They tended to stay away, trying to hold me out with strong arms. This opened up greater opportunities for *uchimata* and *ouchi-gari* than *osoto-gari*.

However, I trusted my *osoto-gari* more than any other technique and I tried it whenever possible. I do not really know why. I have often found a sense of total commitment which I find missing in other throws such as *uchimata*

and *ouchi-gari* which, to a certain extent, involve catching an opponent unawares. With a powerful *osoto-gari,* however, the thrower brushes aside an attempt at a defence and, having got into position, can put 100 per cent of his body and his emotion into one attacking movement, crashing his opponent flat on his back.

I have also enjoyed the danger it represents: while there are few throws more dramatic or powerful than *osoto-gari,* it also can go very wrong, concluding in a 100 per cent counter. But this, to me, is the beauty of judo.

Shunen – Total commitment to one's purpose

A History of Osoto-Gari

The basic principle of stepping towards an opponent and projecting him backwards by reaping a leg seems to have been quite common in many of the older ju-jitsu schools in Japan, though it went under a variety of names. The Tenshin Shinyo Ryu, founded in the early years of the Edo period, in the 17th century, by Mataemon Isoh called it 'kaeri-nage' or 'return throw' and illustrated it in the school's secret scrolls as a man, pulled backwards by an opponent standing behind him, swivelling round and executing *osoto-gari.*

In a collection of techniques from the Seki-guchi Ryu, the *osoto-gari* is demonstrated in another manner. A samurai starts to draw his sword but is blocked when it is just half-way out of the scabbard, pushed off-balance backwards and then thrown with a standard *osoto-gari* entry and reap. This makes it quite clear that *osoto-gari* was regarded as an effective technique, to be employed on the battlefield, with proponents in armour as well as for more general use.

There are records in yet another old collec-

Osoto-gari was regarded as a useful technique against a variety of attacks even in the pre-judo days of ju-jitsu, as these drawings from an old ju-jitsu scroll show. Osoto-gari could clearly be used against opponents with short sleeves — the somewhat stylised representation does not diminish the efficacy of the techniques. An osoto-gari defence used against an opponent grabbing the hair.

tion that the throw was given the name *gyakyu gama* which means 'reverse scythe' which comes much closer to its modern term. After all, gari, the reap, describes the action of the scythe which, when used in the fields, draws a line like an arc. Though the plane of the arc in *osoto-gari* is different to that of *kosoto-gari* or *ouchi-gari*, the basic shape drawn in the air by the attacking leg is the same.

So while Jigoro Kano, who formally inaugurated his Kodokan Judo system in 1882, developed some techniques of his own, *osoto-*

Osoto-gari, apparently, even came in handy if you were attacked by a samurai with two swords — though you had to be quick.

Note the unusual gripping: it is close to the kind of grips seen in modern judo, particularly from Russians.

gari was one which he incorporated from other schools. Hajime Isogai, 10th Dan, suggested in his memoirs, written in the 1930s, that Kano took *osoto-gari* from his studies of the Tozuka School. This suggests a certain irony, because most of the members of the Tokyo Police, who lost the memorable match against the Kodokan shortly after its formation, were from the Tozuka Ryu itself. But it seems clear that *osoto-gari* goes back to well before the Edo period, and may be one of the oldest of the ju-jitsu techniques.

Just how important *osoto-gari* was considered to be by Kano can be seen by the fact that he included it in the first section of the first Gokyo he formulated in Meiji 28 (it was the

(a) The powerful Frenchman Michael Nowak, attacks with osoto-gari, *taking the back of the jacket in an attempt to force his opponent backwards. The technique, at the Tournoi de Paris 1988, failed to score.*

13

second technique) and retained it in the revision he made in 1920, placing it eighth. It remains unknown why he did not include it in *nage-no-kata* (the lack of a backward throw has been regarded as something of a curiosity for decades) but it appears in *kime-no-kata,* as the second technique, called *sode-tori.* It is not unlike the *kaeri-nage* of the Tenshin Shinyo Ryu. Uke attacks tori by grabbing his sleeve. Tori kicks down at uke's knee, swivels round and throws with *osoto-gari.* A form of it also appears in the last set of *ju-no-kata* and in the self-defence kata, *goshin-jitsu-no-kata,* in both cases as a response to a blow.

It certainly featured in competitions in Japan from the early days. Yoshiaki Yamashita, who was the strongest champion in the first years of the Kodokan, and Shuji Nagaoka, the 10th Dan, jointly attested its importance. In a book containing their observations on judo, published by the Kodokan, they described *osoto-gari* as 'one of the most beautiful techniques in judo.' Discussing the technique, they pointed out that it was based on a very natural idea — even when children play at judo or wrestling they often come up with a form of *osoto-gari* without formal instruction. Despite this, it proved so important in competitions from the start of Kodokan Judo, that, they said, it was one of the techniques that everyone had to study.

One of its fiercest exponents just before the Second World War was Masahiko Kimura, who was regarded as one of the most important fighters in the history of judo. He won the All-Japan Championships on three consecutive occasions, before the war interrupted his career, and when he returned to competition in 1949, despite being of advanced age and relatively light at just over 80kg, he won again. *Osoto-gari,* which he practised in a style which is rarely seen, featured prominently in his wins.

The post-war period produced a host of *osoto-gari* specialists. A leading figure was Yasuichi Matsumoto, a tall fighter by Japanese standards at 1.87m. He won the first All-Japan Championships to be held after the war, in Tokyo, in 1948. He swept through the opposition, generally using *osoto-gari.* In six contests, he scored no fewer than four ippons with the technique, including the opening contest against Tomo Komo. It is interesting to note that of the forty-one matches in the event, there were twelve ippon scores from *osoto-gari,* only four from *tsuri-komi-goshi,* two from *uchimata* and one apiece from *seoi-nage, harai-goshi* and other throws. In the whole competition, there were just seven *yusei-gachi* and, with only ippon being scored, these must have included several *waza-ari* scores as well as the *yuko* and *koka* of the modern era.

Matsumoto's height fitted the standard description of an *osoto-gari* specialist and his long legs were seen to be an advantage, but his height was also a disadvantage, for early in his career he found that while he could achieve a good contact with his right leg, the opponents often slipped away under his right armpit. He developed an ingenious answer to this: bending his wrist upward and catching his opponent under the jaw-bone. This effectively prevented the opponent from ducking under his arm and, at the same time, pushed him backwards onto one heel, rendering the reap a relatively simple affair.

This solution was an important advance for *osoto-gari.* It created an *osoto-gari* tradition in Tenri University where Matsumoto trained and, later, taught. A series of outstanding exponents of the throw emerged over the years, including Kazuhiro Ninomiya who won the Olympic light-heavyweight title in 1976 and the World Open title in 1973. The wrist action also appeared as a similarly useful tool for Tenri players specialising in other throws. Sasahara, who won the world light-heavyweight title twice in 1969 and 1971 threw mainly with *uchimata,* using the raised wrist action, though he also produced quite a few *osoto-gari* throws for ippon in his career.

14

Similarly, another Tenri student, Yoshimi Masaki, who won the World Open title in 1985, has used the raised wrist with *harai-goshi*, though again he sometimes switched to *osoto-gari* when the situation demanded.

Although it is usually wrong to generalise, it is possible to suggest that three main *osoto-gari* styles have emerged over the years.

Moving Style

This style is based on a sleeve/middle lapel grip, or possibly two lapels, but the principal feature is that it uses a flexible movement pattern. Tori allies speed to a subtle *kuzushi* obtained by alert use of his hands to make his entry and put his opponent into a position where he can be reaped easily. The use of the hands is crucial, but combinations also often play an important role. Difficult to describe precisely in words, it is easier to categorise in terms of specialists. This was Daigo's style and it is my style also. The two finalists in the open category of the Los Angeles Olympic games, Hitoshi Saito and Angelo Parisi, also belong to this style. Bernard Tchoullyan, the French middleweight, is another example.

Raised Wrist (Tenri) Style

This was Matsumoto's style, and while not exclusively used by fighters from Tenri University, it is interesting how the university has produced one generation after another of *osoto-gari* exponents who use this method extensively, even when, as in the case of Masaki who is not particularly tall, physical attributes militate against it. In addition to Matsumoto, Ninomiya and Masaki practise this style.

Power Style

Exponents of this style form a large group encompassing *osoto-gari* specialists who

(a) Kimura attacks with tremendous flair and panache, sending his reaping leg high in the air to gather optimum momentum.

appear very different but who base their breaking of the balance on one powerful pull with the *tsurite* (lapel or collar) grip. Often they take a high collar grip and pull their opponent tight into the chest, helping with the sleeve grip. Sometimes, like Kimara, they manage to make this strong chest contact with the lapel grip.

Into this category fall fighters as varied as Isamu Sonoda (Japan), Wilhelm Ruska (Holland), Hiroshi Minatoya, World Champion in 1967 and 1969, Chonuske Takagi, Sergey Novikov (Soviet Union), Robert van de Walle (Belgium), David Starbrook (Britain), Takehide Nakatani, and Peter Seisenbacher (Austria).

There have been times when *osoto-gari* has fallen into disfavour at the top level of international competition, but it has always recovered and emerged stronger than before in the hands of a new champion. It is a constant feature of randori practice world-wide.

Osto-Gari

Techniques

Standard judo lore dictates that *osoto-gari* is a throw used mainly by middleweights and above and that it is classically the province of the taller, heavier fighter. The fundamental aim of the technique is to put the opponent on the back of his heels and then reap away his feet. It does not take an engineer to work out how much easier this is for the taller of two opponents. Many smaller men have devised ways of overcoming this problem over the years and in any case the use of weight categories should have made this rule somewhat obsolete, but they do remain the exception.

There are a number of reasons why *osoto-gari* is seen more frequently in middleweight judo and above, but perhaps the most important one is posture. Middleweight men and above tend to stand upright, however unorthodox their grip, or certainly more upright than the lighter classes who work from a more varied posture. It is very difficult, even for an *osoto-gari* specialist, to throw an opponent bent in a *jigotai* (defensive position). It is almost a requirement of *osoto-gari* that the basic posture of at least the person being thrown is reasonably upright.

(a) and (b) The Tenri style of osoto-gari *perfectly illustrated by Masaki, the 1985 World Open Weight Champion, against Haga in the 1986 All-Japan Championships.*

The first photograph demonstrates the none-too-gentle 'push' from the wrist to achieve the break of balance. The second photograph shows just how effective the manoeuvre was.

Basic Technique (Fig 1)

Keynote

The movement should be relatively fast but smooth. Control is more important than speed though, as they settle in to the technique.

(a) I face my opponent in *hon shizentai,* a relaxed upright posture. The grip is left against left, the technical Japanese term being *ai-yotsu.*

(b) For demonstration purposes, I have taken two steps backwards (left then right) in order to be able to initiate the kind of movement pattern that I would create in a contest or randori. This is the way I do my basic *uchi-komi.*

(c) I take a big step with my right foot, slightly pulling myself on to my opponent with my left hand. As I draw level with him, my right hand brings his sleeve down to my side, ideally towards my belt, although it rarely gets as close as that. My left forearm starts to push against his shoulder.

(d) I point my toe, creating the start of a strong power curve.

(e) I start to lower my head and, at the same time, reap with my left leg. Note how uke is bent over backwards.

(f) My head goes down and my foot comes up in a classic see-saw action. This can generate considerable power.

(g) The finish of the throw.

Important Points

The Feet (Fig 2)

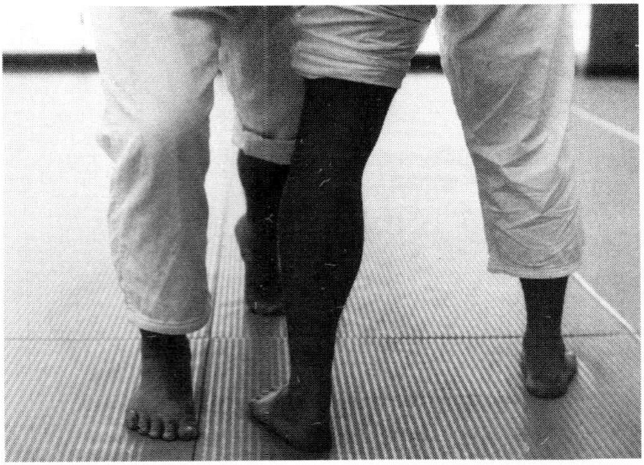

(a) I want to leave a gap the width of one foot between my opponent's foot and my supporting leg. The toes of my right foot are pointing forwards. They indicate the direction of the throw, which, in this case, is backwards.

(c) How not to do it – if I jab at my opponent's leg like this, the action will be jagged and restricted in its range.

Note   At this stage, the weight on my standing leg should be on the ball of my foot, slightly more on the inner side than the outer. My heel is on the ground, but there is very little weight on it. Of course, the knee is bent. It must not feel stiff and robotic but springy and alive, in order to give dynamism to the whole technique.

(b) I point the toes of the reaping leg. I want a smooth powerful action throughout the range of movement.

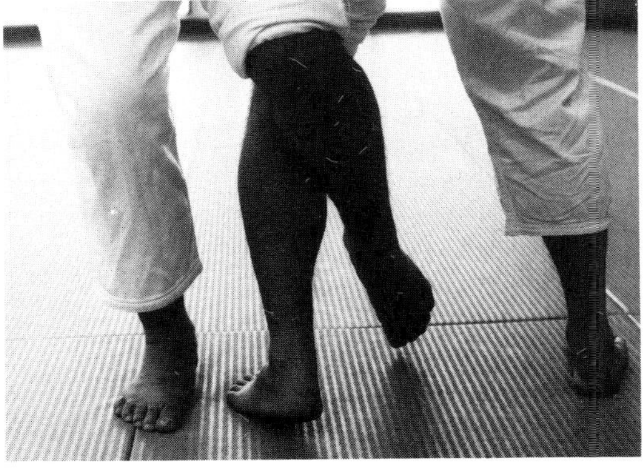

(d) The reap. I have pulled up the trousers to make the point of contact very clear. The top of my calf makes contact with the top of my opponent's calf. It has the effect of collapsing his leg when his weight is extended over it, and he is bending backwards.

Kuzushi – Breaking of Balance (Fig 3)

(a) The ideal position into which I am trying to put my opponent. Once he is leaning back a little, like the Leaning Tower of Pisa, the sweeping motion is simple. This is not easy to achieve, but it is a major part of the throw.

(b) I want to get my opponent in this position, with virtually all his weight travelling down to his left heel. I do this by simultaneously pulling his sleeve towards my side with my right hand, and pushing against his upper chest and shoulder with my left forearm and hand. If the opponent was taken away, you would see my hands making a simultaneous action in opposing directions. This is the real secret of the *kuzushi,* and it is not easy to master. However, once it is acquired, it gives excellent control of the opponent.

There is generally a slight gap between my chest and my opponent, but the hands are controlling well.

Osoto-Gari Against a Smaller Opponent (Fig 4)

(a) My opening movement is the same as the basic *osoto-gari*. (The camera angle makes me look smaller, but this is not the case.)

(c) I turn my wrist and pull his sleeve and arm across my chest. This time I want good chest contact. The effect of this action is to pin my opponent on his left leg, the one I intend to reap.

Keynote

The smaller opponent is probably, though not always, faster, and will find it relatively easy to whip the attacked leg out of my reach. So, my *kuzushi* has got to prevent this or at least give me such control of him that I can restrict his movement and get the leg in the end.

(b) My body may bend a little if the difference in heights is acute, but I want to keep as upright as I can in order not to shorten the reaping arc. This is one reason why I start a different pulling action with my right hand. Instead of pulling to my side, I start to pull outwards.

(d) and (e) The rest follows as usual with the see-saw action putting my opponent on his back.

(f) This close-up shows the important difference. The final twist on the wrist brings my chest into full contact with my opponent. It can feel a bit like a ratchet clicking into place. The left hand, the *tsurite* or lapel grip hand, works in the same manner as for the basic *osoto-gari*.

Osoto-Gari Against a Taller and Heavier Opponent (Fig 5)

Keynote

In this technique, the crucial part is played by the *tsurite* hand (the lapel grip) as this sequence, taken from the rear angle, illustrates clearly.

(a) I take a slightly lower grip on my opponent's lapel with my left hand, abiding by the basic rule of not reaching up more than feels naturally comfortable. The higher up I reach with the left hand, the weaker my power resource on that arm.

(b) My entry is standard.

(c) As I start to come into line with my opponent, my left elbow comes across a little, just in front of me. My right hand, on his sleeve, starts to pull towards my side as in the basic style although, because he is taller, it will feel to him as if the pull is more directly down.

(d) I pick up his chin with my knuckles. The feeling can also be described as placing the knuckles under the chin. A careless movement can be a little unpleasant for the opponent. As the whole action progresses towards the throw, my opponent's chin is pushed further into the air. It is tempting to describe it as a punch, to give the idea of pushing firmly, but of course judo rules prohibit such as attack. However, as the fingers still maintain their grip on the lapel, it is surprising how much force can be put into the action without finding that one is treading a thin line . . .

(e)–(g) The throwing action is the same as usual.

There are various possible placings of the knuckles. Experimentation for personal preference is called for.

Osoto-Gari Using a High Collar Grip (Fig 6)

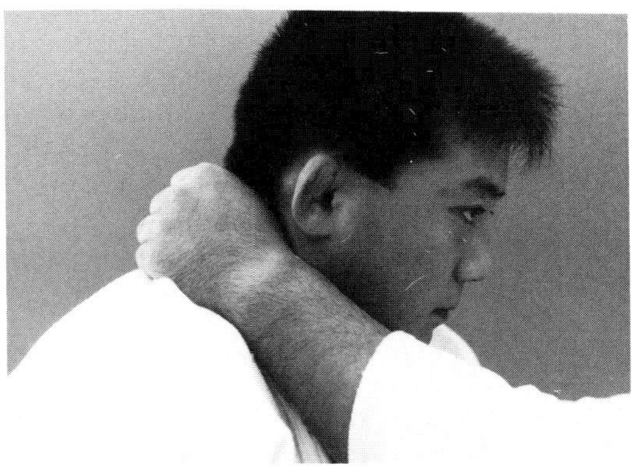

(a) The grip. The thumb is inside the collar. The wrist is turned so that the little finger is down, giving me control of my opponent's shoulder and upper chest with my wrist and forearm.

Keynote

This is now the most common *osoto-gari*. Its advantage is that it is much easier than the basic or traditional style which calls for a more subtle use of the *tsurite* (lapel grip) hand to obtain a useful *kuzushi*. However, t is more limited in its use. It can really only be used against a smaller opponent, or perhaps against an opponent of the same height, and it does not offer the same range of combinations, restricting the user to throws such as *harai-goshi* or *uchimata*. This is the grip used by most heavyweights now.

(b) When I pull in, my elbow bends to less than a right-angle. I want to pull him in close so that I can obtain good contact and total head control.

(c) This is aided by using the same sleeve (*hikite*) pull as in the technique against the smaller opponent. I pull the sleeve and arm across my chest, turning my wrist to 'click' it in place.

26

(d) and (e) The throw. As I attack, I want to remain quite lively and relaxed in my total body movement despite tightening up at the top. I turn the right wrist to gain control.

(f)–(h) My chest makes contact and my opponent's balance is broken. I ensure that the reaping leg comes straight up as normal and does not veer to the right – which would reduce reaping power.

(i) and (j) The throw is taken slightly at an angle because of my strong pull on the sleeve.

The Raised Wrist – Tenri Style (Fig 7)

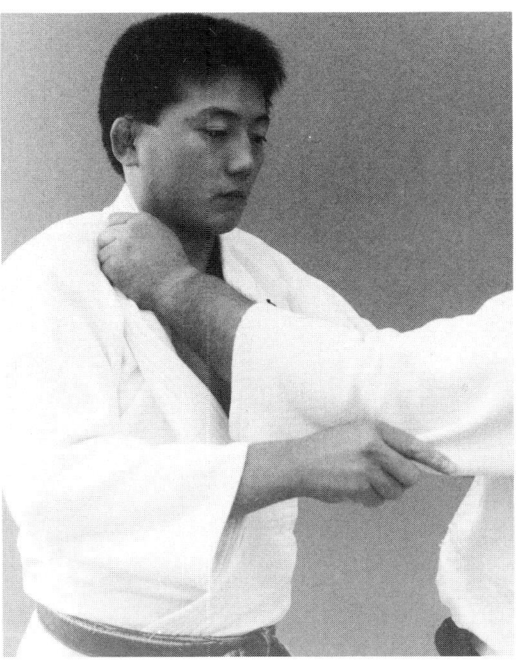

(a) The wrist action. I take quite a high grip on the lapel, but not at the back of the neck. My left arm must be quite relaxed.

Keynote

This seems to be a small detail, but it has proved remarkably versatile not only in its use in *osoto-gari* attacks against smaller, equal size and even (a little) taller opponents, but also in other techniques such as *harai-goshi* and *uchi-mata*. It is clearly worth considering, not least because it has been used consistently by Tenri fighters – and others – since it was developed, by Yasuichi Matsumoto, in the 1940s.

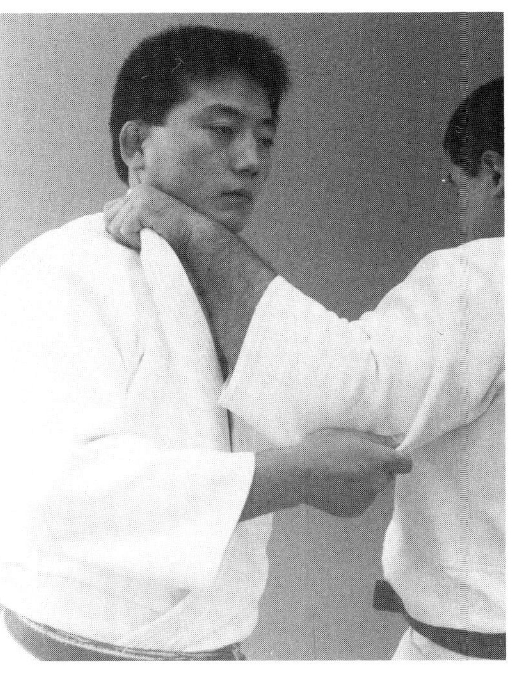

(b) I raise my wrist. I want the top part of the hand, at the base of thumb and forefinger, to make contact just under my opponent's jaw.

(c) This has the important effect of pushing my opponent's head backwards, with a consequent effect on his balance. I can achieve a surprising amount of control and even power from this very simple movement.

(d) and (e) I launch myself at my opponent. Notice that he is bending forward slightly as I pull myself in.

(f) The effect of the raised wrist can be quite dramatic, as here, flicking his head backwards and putting him in the ideal position for *osoto-gari*.

(g) When the balance has been broken so effectively, very little power is needed from the reaping leg.

(h) This side view shows how heavy, and even potentially dangerous, a fall from *osoto-gari* can be. It is not a throw to be used without control, especially against much weaker or lighter opponents or randori partners.

Osoto-Gari – Kenka-Yotsu Style (Fig 8)

Keynote

When a left hander faces a right hander, the *osoto-gari* specialist is presented with a slightly more difficult test. The opposing stances place the leg to be attacked some distance away, and in between is often a strongly defensive fist burrowing in against the shoulder preventing a smooth and natural entry. However, once the entry has been made, and the defences broken, the throw can be very hard indeed. Uke resists totally until the last second, when suddenly he crashes to the mat.

(a) The opposing stance. I start my movement

(b) I step in with my right leg in much the same manner as for the basic *osoto-gari*, my hands contributing by pulling myself in with the help of my opponent's body.

(c) As I close on him, I start the twisting action with my hands.

(d) This twisting action is now in an intermediate stage. As my reaping leg gets into position for the attack, my right hand is pulling his sleeve into my side while my right hand is pushing against the side of his neck. The *kuzushi* is beginning to take place. If I start to push and pull any earlier, my opponent will probably manage to take his leg back, well out of reach.

30

(e) and (f) I completed the breaking of the balance at the same time as I made contact with the reaping leg. It is very clear now that the throw is on. And my opponent is toppled like a tree.

Variation (Fig 9)

Keynote

This happens often, particularly at international events. It has proved impossible to close the space between myself and my opponent sufficiently to get into an ideal *osoto-gari* position before the reaping leg comes into action. What to do?

(a) I have taken the step with my right foot but, because of the forceful response of my opponent, my right foot is placed at a different angle. (Sometimes, it appears as if I have taken a backstep with my right foot.) Almost simultaneously, my left foot goes over my opponent's right, like a hook.

(b) It is crucial, once this position is reached, that I do not relax the pulling/reaping motion with my left leg. I have not just hooked in and allowed it to rest lightly over my opponent's leg; I am actively working it, concentrating on it the whole time, trying unceasingly to reap the leg. This cannot be stressed too often. If I relax that leg, it is an easy matter for my opponent to twist slightly and throw with *osoto-gaeshi*. I can help to prevent this by leaning in with my head and upper body. Of course, my hands are working too — my right pulling, my left pushing to get a twisting action.

(c) and (d) I hop round. It looks as if all of my weight is on my right leg, but a sizeable amount is on the left reaping leg. Not only does this help to pull me round into a throwing position, but it also ensures that my opponent is pinned to the ground and cannot counter.

Although I came in at an angle, I am now turning round to attain a proper position for a throw. If I try to throw at the angle in Fig 13(b), it will be a hopeless task. He is relatively strong to the side, but weaker to the back. Having made the semi-circle, the *osoto-gari* is now possible.

Osoto-gake (major outer hook) (Fig 10)

Keynote

Jean-Luc Rouge, the French 1975 world champion, put his long legs to good advantage as can be seen in his demonstration of osoto-gake. This technique enabled him to cover the considerable gap in a kenka-yotsu situation.

(a) The gripping is mixed, but the basic stance is kenka-yotsu. Rouge takes the over-grip with the left hand. This is a crucial element of the throw: Rouge puts weight on uke's right arm as he attacks which helps to pin his opponent on the right foot.

(b) He takes a wide step with his left leg — stepping away in a manner which suggests harai-goshi more than osoto-gari.

(c) This harai-goshi feint becomes more pronounced with the initial hip movement. The right shoulder here also suggests a turning motion like harai-goshi.

(d) Suddenly, the direction of the throw changes. Rouge throws his right leg out in osoto-gari fashion. Note the relaxed and bent left leg.

(e) The attacking foot snakes behind uke's right leg. It doesn't just rest there, but starts to apply pressure.

(f) The positioning of the attacking leg – tori's calf pushing into the back of the knee – makes uke sink.

The use of the hands are very important. The right (hidden) hand is using a Tenri-style push, with the wrist bent and pushing against the head. The left hand pulls in tighter. These two actions together, plus the "sinking" effect of the attacking right leg, breaks uke's balance and makes him bend backwards.

(g) Rouge takes another step with the left foot, hooking hard all the time with his right leg. Then, once in place for the final throwing action, he raises his right leg again.

(h) Now, he reaps to throw.

Note: Rouge comments: This technique enabled me to attack with osoto-gari when my opponent thought it was impossible to attack. The element of surprise is very strong.

Obi-Tori-Osoto-Gari (Fig 11)

Keynote

This technique is not often seen in Japan, but it is used regularly and with great success by many top fighters from the Soviet Union. This may be because, like many belt-grip throws, it is a real power movement — something which the Russians excell at, and which play such a prominent part in their own jacket wrestling style, sambo. Fighters like the World Champions Shota Khabarelli and Khoubculouri became famous for this kind of move, throwing the hand over the shoulder to grab for the belt. I used it once, the first time I won the All-Japan Championships in 1977, throwing Teruo Masaki because, in the natural movement of contest, I saw the opportunity and took it. But I did not plan to go for the belt, as the Russians do.

(a) My opponent is defending vigorously by settling into a low *jigotai*, pushing me away

(b) I break grip, pulling away my *tsurite* (lapel grip) hand, stepping back to do so.

Note Big and powerful players can choose between *osoto-gari* and *harai-goshi* once they have the belt, but if faced with an opponent of equal stature and power, it may be better to stay with the *osoto-gari*. It is used in many international competitions, and at all weights.

(c) I do not go over the head, but reach through, past the side of the head for the belt. This is safer and means there is less likelihood of a counter. As soon as my hand grips the belt – thumb in, if possible, not just the fingers – I take an extra step with my right foot, like a conventional *osoto-gari*.

(d) My hip comes through, and I can reap relatively easily, pulling my opponent backwards with the help of the belt.

(e) Having reaped, I will inevitably find myself going down to the ground with my opponent because of my belt grip. It can be a rather heavy experience for my opponent. Maybe next time, he will not resort to *jigotai* to stop the *osoto-gari* attack.

Osoto-Gari With Ippon-Seoi Variation (Fig 12)

Keynote

This is another variation which is often seen in international competition when competitors are well attuned to defences against both *ippon-seoi-nage* and *osoto-gari*. This mixture of both can prove extremely effective (It is demonstrated by two students of mine at Tokai University.)

(a) This is a *kenka-yotsu* situation, with both holding the lapel grip. Ideally, tori has the top grip.

(b) Tori steps back a little, pulling his opponent onto his right leg.

(c) This makes it easier for tori to spin into the *osoto-gari* position, but with his left arm in *ippon-seoi* position.

(d) and (e) Although this often does not feel very dangerous to the opponent, he is suddenly taken off balance as tori brings his shoulder into play. The throw is easy.

(f) This is what it looks like from the other side.

(g) Tori has taken his left arm down.

(a) Nobuyuki Sato throws his opponent with ippon/osoto, *bringing down his right hand at the last second to aid the reaping action.*

Timing

The Opponent Steps Backwards — The Chase (Fig 13)

(a) I start a movement pattern. Timing is about catching the opponent on the move. This can vary in judo from a miniscule movement — more an adjustment of balance than anything else — to a bold multi-step pattern. I am demonstrating this timing in this manner, though of course, in contest, a much shortened version is more likely to occur. I create movement by pushing on the sleeve grip and putting my whole body into a stepping pattern.

(c) As his left foot starts to go backwards, I take a large, bold step with my right foot.

Keynote

This is the most successful timing used by most of the *osoto-gari* specialists, including myself. It is the first timing everyone should learn, not least because it is the most useful — and the easiest. It works with virtually all the versions of *osoto-gari*.

(b) My opponent's reaction is to retreat a few steps. I keep step with him, trying to control his body with my hands, but without telegraphing the fact to him. Such control is a subtle business. Suddenly, I break the rhythm.

(d) As I move into the attack I start to break his balance, in this case by taking my knuckles under his chin forcing his head back — the smaller man's *osoto-gari*.

40

(e) and (f) My opponent is now pinned on his back foot. There is nowhere for him to go but down.

(g)–(i) Which he duly does.

Dehana (Fig 14)

Keynote

Dehana means 'just advanced' and describes this timing perfectly. It can be regarded as a high-level technique, and because it depends on quite a relaxed movement it is not often seen in top contest, though when it is, it is spectacular. The timing is so perfect that the technique feels as light as an *okuri-ashi-barai*, with almost no effort involved.

(a) Once again, I create a movement pattern, imposing my wish upon my opponent without letting him know that I am luring him into a technique. I push him backwards for a couple of steps or so. In competition this is rarely possible, but it is more possible in randori. To be learned, it must be done with a co-operative partner, at first, to develop the feeling.

(b) and (c) My opponent has had enough and stops retreating, perhaps suddenly realising that he is being manipulated. He begins to push forwards.

(d) Almost anticipating the change, my left foot has taken half a pace backwards in time with my opponent's right foot coming forwards. This gives me the little space I need to create my attacking power movement. I spring forwards, coming off my back foot.

(e) At virtually the same time, my opponent has stepped forward on his left foot, and it is a relatively simple matter to sweep past him and get into the *osoto-gari* position. The basic idea is that my opponent has stepped into the throw totally unaware of what is about to happen.

(f) and (g) Just as he is about to put his weight on his left foot, my left leg reaps. The effect — the up-ending of my opponent — is instantaneous.

Note   This is the perfect, classic way for a small person to throw a large person with *osoto-gari*, not least because the smaller person should have the advantage of speed and manoeuvrability. When it happens, you can throw an opponent weighing 100kg or more, and he will only feel like 40kg.

The Tricks

Keynote

There have always been tricks in judo and every top competitor has his little battery of tricks, often involving his *tokui waza* which he can bring out from time to time. Here are a couple, using the same principle of stepping on the opponent's foot — not particularly elegant, but it can be useful.

Trick 1 (Fig 15)

Keynote

This was used by a Korean fighter in the Kano Cup in 1982. He threw the powerful Russian fighter, Alexander Iastkevich, twice for *yuko*, and was leading until the last minute when he was armlocked (though that had a controversial element too as the Korean claimed he had not submitted).

(a) Standing with normal grips, tori surreptitiously steps on uke's right foot with his left foot.

(b) Uke is a little confused and, failing to take his right foot away, steps back on his left.

(c) and (d) Taking good control of the upper body, tori steps across for the *osoto-gari*, and reaps.

Trick 2 (Fig 16)

Keynote

The same idea, but with the other foot.

(a) Standing square.

(b) Tori just steps across and plants his right foot on uke's right foot.

(c) Once again, uke, a little confused, tries to regain balance and pull away.

(d) The momentary restriction on uke's movement allows tori to step in to place for *osoto-gari* in the orthodox manner. For this to work, tori must control uke's upper body.

The *osoto-gari* then follows as normal.

Renzokuwaza – Combination Techniques

Combinations

Combinations have always been an integral part of judo. They fulfil the basic philosophy of judo of maximum efficiency with minimum effort. An attack produces a strong defence, but the second attack capitalises on that very defensive action and over the opponent goes onto his back. Some of the most beautiful judo emerges from these varied movement patterns, in contrast to the more direct power of the single, all-out attack.

There are various kinds of combination. First of all there is *renrakuwaza*, the true combination. I attack with one technique but it is just a feint, a device to elicit a particular response from my opponent. In basic parlance, I want to set him up. Once he is in a particular position, I can produce the main throw. Secondly, there is *renzokuwaza*, where I attack with real commitment at the start, and, because of my opponent's reaction, I find myself going into a second technique.

Sometimes one kind is appropriate; sometimes the other will work best. On other occasions, the combination is prepared during the course of a contest. I attack with *osoto-gari* a few times, nearly scoring, and then switch. It is possible to effect a combination over different rounds. An opponent sees me throw with one technique in the first round and expects that I will try the same in the second round against him. I make a feint and he duly defends, but I switch to something different and totally unexpected.

Combinations work in different ways within the technical range of judo, but by and large it is a question of opposites. It could be forward and backward, like *osoto-gari* to *tai-otoshi*, or left to right, or inside to outside like *ouchi-gari* to *osoto-gari*. The fascination of combinations is that there are endless permutations, some classic and long-lasting and others made to work in the hands of just one or two people.

Yet, for the past two decades, combinations have not been used as frequently as direct attacks at the top international competitions. This may be partly due to the nature of modern competition itself. Winning is all-important, so caution plays a large part in a contest. It is much safer for a fighter to attack and, if it fails, come out and start again from a secure position than to continue and risk everything in a different movement.

Another factor may be the size of the judogi. If you look at the size of the jackets on the participants in the Tokyo Olympics and compare them to the jackets on the participants in the Seoul Olympics, you will see that the closely fitted jackets of Seoul made gripping very difficult. Often, it would be possible to get a grip to make an attack, but, if the attack was not successful, the opponent was able to break the grip to defend against further danger until he had resumed his balance. The changes in the rules governing the size of jackets, in 1990, may result in a comeback for combinations in top competitions.

However, combinations have always been used in randori where the tensions are less, and they are part of the repertoire of skills of any able judoka. *Osoto-gari* is a technique which offers a wide range of combinations and the following are just a selection of the most important.

Osoto-Gari into Ouchi-Gari (Major Outer Reap into Major Inner Reap) (Fig 17)

Keynote

This is unquestionably the most common *osoto-gari* combination in both contest and randori. While it can be used against opponents with the same-sided grip, I have found it particularly effective in the *kenka-yotsu* situation. The special angle created when two players come together with opposing grips provides an excellent opportunity.

(a) This is a feint combination. I know I am intending to change to *ouchi-gari* but my initial approach must be identical to my normal *osoto-gari*.

(b) I step forward with my right foot as usual.

(c) I start my *kuzushi,* pulling a little on the sleeve grip. I need to ensure that my opponent is sufficiently worried about the impending *osoto-gari* to take his left foot away in a sharp, defensive motion.

However, I must not get too close — I must leave a gap in which I can turn in the opposite direction.

(d) This is where I switch to *ouchi-gari*. I know that I am changing, but my opponent is still not aware of my intention.

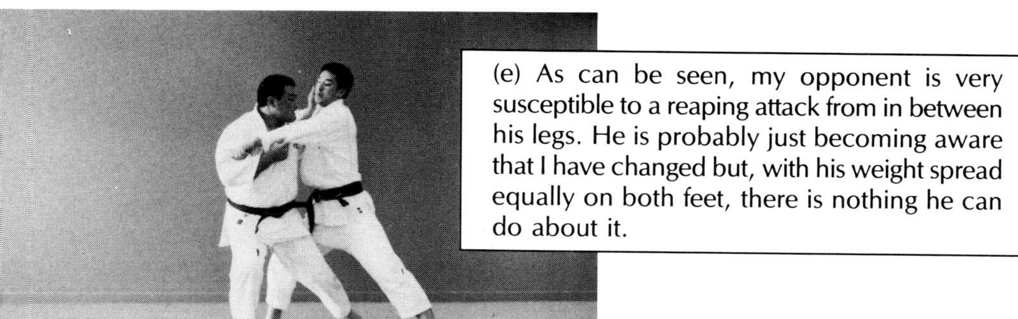

(e) As can be seen, my opponent is very susceptible to a reaping attack from in between his legs. He is probably just becoming aware that I have changed but, with his weight spread equally on both feet, there is nothing he can do about it.

(f)–(h) As I reap, I want to make my opponent do the splits. This is not a traditional semi-circle reaping action – my opponent's position does not require that. He just needs his legs to be separated a little more, and then it is a simple matter to put him on his back.

Osoto-Gari to Sasae-Tsuri-Komi-Ashi (Fig 18)

Keynote

This is usually best executed from a static position, or perhaps when the opponent is coming forward. It is best done from an *ai-yotsu* grip, but *kenka-yotsu* is also possible.

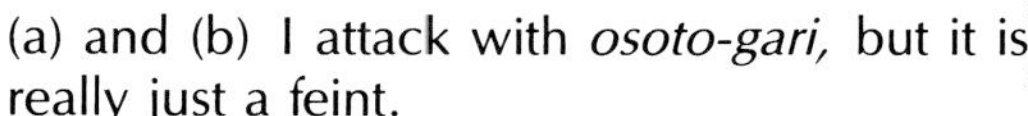

(a) and (b) I attack with *osoto-gari,* but it is really just a feint.

(c) I take the first step, but I am preparing to change position. I break the balance, pulling with my right hand, but I do not begin to bring my left leg through for the *osoto-gari*. Notice, however, that I am still looking ahead, as if I really was going to do *osoto-gari*.

(d) I switch to *sasae-tsuri-komi-ashi,* my left leg starting to come up to block. My opponent is leaning forward in the direction I want to take him.

(e) Almost simultaneously, my hands come into play. They switch direction, the right hand pushing up on my opponent's arm and the left hand pulling down on his collar. The leg is now firmly in place.

(f)–(h) Over he goes. Notice the way he lands — my left hand, the *tsurite* hand, has pulled him right round.

Note In the semi-final of the World Championships in Paris in 1979, I threw the tall Russian, Turin, with exactly this technique. Precisely ten years later, in the selection contests for the Japanese team, Naoya Ogawa, the 1987 World Open champion, who was to go on to retain the title in Belgrade in 1989, threw his main domestic rival, Hideyuki Sekine, in the same way, also for ippon.

Osoto-Gari into Uchimata (Fig 19)

Keynote

This is another combination which works particularly well against an opponent with opposing grips. It helps to take the inside grip with the *tsurite* hand.

(a) I stand in the characteristic *kenka-yotsu* position.

(b) I start to attack, taking a short step backwards with my left foot to gather momentum.

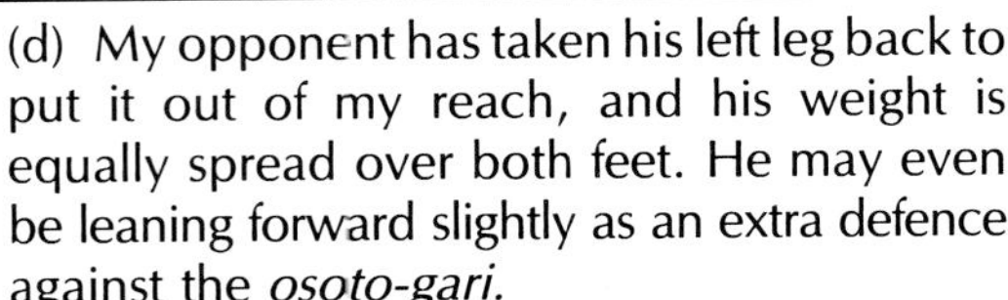

(c) I step into the *osoto-gari* pattern. The *osoto-gari* has just been a feint. At this stage, my opponent still thinks that the *osoto-gari* is coming, but as I bring my left leg through, I know I am going to switch to an *uchimata*.

(d) My opponent has taken his left leg back to put it out of my reach, and his weight is equally spread over both feet. He may even be leaning forward slightly as an extra defence against the *osoto-gari*.

(e) I pivot on my supporting leg, turning in the space, and attack with *uchimata*.

(f) and (g) In this demonstration, I have taken my opponent into the air, but sometimes, in competition or randori, it is necessary to throw using *ken-ken uchimata*, making one or two hops on my supporting leg to turn him on his back.

(h) and (i) The throw.

Note   This device can be used against smaller opponents who you want to throw with *uchimata* but who use *uchimata sukashi* (the avoidance and counter of *uchimata*). These opponents tend to put their weight onto their left foot if they are expecting an *uchimata* attack from that side. However, the *osoto-gari* feint forces them to open their legs suddenly and it is then possible to throw with *uchimata*.

Osoto-Gari to Tai-Otoshi (Fig 20)

Keynote

This is particularly useful for fighters faced with heavier opponents. Of course, the one-sided grip must not be held for more than a few seconds in contest.

(a) I hold the sleeve with my right hand, and the lapel on the same side with my left. I can afford to be fairly static, although it also works well on the move.

(b) I bring my leg across.

(c) I hook my opponent's leg just behind the knee, exerting just a little pressure on his leg — enough to make him think that I really am going to try and throw him backwards.

(d) Now I switch to *tai-otoshi*. Holding just one side of the judogi enables me to slip into the tai-otoshi position quite easily.

(e) I am aiming to throw him, not directly to the front as in a classic *tai-otoshi,* but, partly because of the grip, slightly to one side.

(f)–(h) From here, it is not difficult to turn him on his back.

Ouchi-Gari into Osoto-Gari (Fig 21)

(a) and (b) I attack with *ouchi-gari*.

(c) Even as I come in, I can sense that my opponent has managed to keep a little weight off his right leg, and will simply lift it off and away to safety.

Keynote

In competitions, when I attacked with *ouchi-gari,* it was always with full commitment. If my opponent escaped, it felt quite natural to follow through with *osoto-gari.*

(d) Unimpeded, my reaping foot has returned to its starting position, but the attack has set another pattern in motion. My opponent has started to retreat and I find myself in precisely the starting position I like for my main *osoto-gari* attack.

(e) This is the timing of the chase. I pull myself in.

(f) I bring his left arm slightly out as I step in, level.

(g) and (h) The *kuzushi* comes into play properly as I bring my leg through.

(i) and (j) Having expected to be attacked from the inside, my opponent now finds him-self taken over with a major outer reap.

Note   This is a basic combination, but it works well even at the highest level because if I make a very hard opening *ouchi-gari* attack, my opponent has no chance to think of what is coming next. He is only glad that he has escaped. He does not realise that he has walked directly into another trap.

Sasae-Tsuri-Komi-Ashi into Osoto-Gari (Fig 22)

Keynote

This is basically a reversal of the earlier combination. These two work well as a pair because the opening step is the same.

(a) and (b) I step in, but I lift his left arm with my sleeve grip and pull down on my lapel grip.

(c) I want to achieve a little turn – just enough to make him concerned about a *sasae-tsuri-komi-ashi.*

(d) He has begun to pull back in defence, and I can move into the *osoto-gari.*

(e) The *kuzushi* is often quite easy to get because he has helped me by pulling away from the *sasae.*

(f) This photograph shows the correct placing of the reaping leg very clearly. This applies to all *osoto-gari* throws.

(g) The throw.

Note   I first appreciated this combination when I was at senior high school. I was fighting in the All-Japan High-School Competition, and in the quarter-final I attacked my opponent three times with *osoto-gari* but I could not throw, so I switched to *sasae-tsuri-komi-ashi* and scored ippon. In the next round, my opponent came out worrying about the *sasae-tsuri-komi-ashi* – I could just sense it – so I feinted the throw, but switched to *osoto-gari.* It was ippon in fifteen seconds.

Kaeshi-Waza – Counters

Defences and Counters

Perhaps because *osoto-gari* involves such a direct attacking line, it can be fairly easy to stop. A deep *jigotai* is enough to discourage even a committed *osoto-gari* specialist, even though some manage to power or deceive their way past the strongest and stiffest of arms. Of course, with the passivity rules, it is difficult for one fighter to spend the whole time defending against the threat of frontal assault. In any case, defending against one throw such as *osoto-gari* opens the way to others.

In the to and fro of contest or randori, an *osoto-gari* specialist will get past the arms, the first line of defence, at least partially. Even then, all is not lost for the defender. There are two areas of strategic importance for the attacker:

1. Chest contact or control of the upper body which allows him to bend his opponent backward for an effective *kuzushi*.
2. The attacking leg needs to come across, either to hook in and allow him to hop his way into a reaping position, or the attacking fighter needs to be able to sweep past his opponent in order to reap him directly.

Stop the Action

Keynote

The basic idea here is to stop the action before it really gets going. The reason why I started most of my attacking movements in the earlier chapters some distance away from my opponent was to build up momentum and make the attack more difficult to stop. Even if my opponent does see me coming in, I can disguise the approach — it could be *osoto-gari* or *ouchi-gari,* or I could be going to switch to *sasae-tsuri-komi-ashi.*

When I am being attacked in such a manner, I can limit the possible damage by a simple hand defence.

(a) A typical tangle from a failed osoto-gari *in the 71kg category at the 1988 Olympics. Stranz (West Germany) has attacked with* osoto-gari, *but has been picked up by Wolwender of Liechtenstein. Stranz immediately hooks in with his right foot to prevent a counter-throw.*

The Wrist Turn (Fig 23)

(a) This is my normal hand position — strong, but relaxed. I am ready to attack or defend.

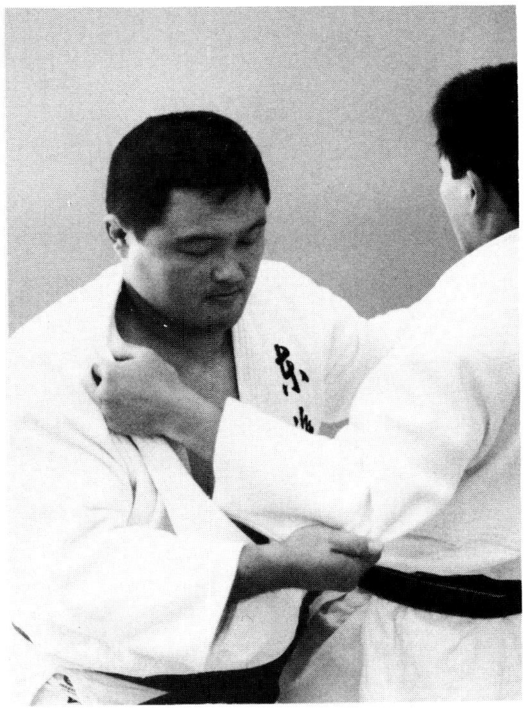

(b) I feel an *oscto-gari* attack coming. My opponent tries to come across to one side. I just turn my wrist and push his elbow away. This acts like a sudden brake on his whole left side and, when done correctly, just kills the movement dead. Its advantage is that it is a very small movement and can be done quickly. Its disadvantage is that if the grip is not secure and the elbow control slips from the grasp, the opponent has an easy passage into the throwing position.

The Step Back (Fig 24)

(a) My opponent readies for an attack.

(b) and (c) As he comes across, my wrist comes into action and simultaneously I drop my weight, taking my left leg, which he needs to reach, well out of range. It appears a simple motion, but practice is needed to drop the weight suddenly and evenly. It is a fast but controlled lowering of the body, not a collapse. This, incidentally, is what I did not manage to do in the Los Angeles Olympics when Laurent del Colombo threw me for a *koka*. My injured leg (it was my right in this case) just could not retreat at the speed at which it would have normally done, and down I went.

It is an indication that it is often not enough just to defend with the hands against a committed and skilful attack.

If my attacker is taller, and has taken a high collar grip, dominating the grips, all that I can do when he starts to attack is take the leg back and sink the weight well. If I do not, I leave myself open for a forward-throw combination.

Sukui-Nage (Scooping Throw) (Fig 25)

Keynote

In my contest career, I used this counter when I was attacked with *osoto-gari* by a left-hander like myself. In other words, in an *ai-yotsu* situation. The technique is known in Japan as *sukui-nage,* and most commonly in the West as *te-guruma* or hand wheel. It is quite an easy technique even though the lift gives it a dramatic character, but it needs to be learned in two stages.

Basic Defence

(a) My opponent initiates his attack.

(b) My first reaction is to stop the action, twisting the wrist and taking my foot back as a simple precaution. When learning *sukui-nage,* it is best to think of this as the first stage. Make the defence, and pause momentarily. The next step is to release the sleeve grip and grasp the inner thigh. The danger is that this is done too quickly, before the initial attack has been stopped properly, and the attacker can simply hook in with his outstretched leg and hop across for the throw.

(c) Having stabilised, and truly stopped the attack, I reach under for the grip. I want to get a secure grip on the leg. It is easier than fumbling for the cloth of the trousers and ensures a higher lift. My hand comes quite far through to curve around the inner thigh, but the actual lifting work is done by the inner forearm.

(d) Basic judo practice teaches me to bring the hips into the lifting work. It is very difficult – and unnecessary – to do it just with the arms like an hydraulic hoist. I do not think of taking my opponent straight up, but more of turning him in a circle, with my left hand on his lapel pulling his head and upper body down and the thigh grip pulling him round in a wheel. Once this action is felt, it is quite easy.

(e) As he comes up high, I move my weight onto my left foot, and turn him around my hip.

(f)–(h) It is then simple to unload him in front of me.

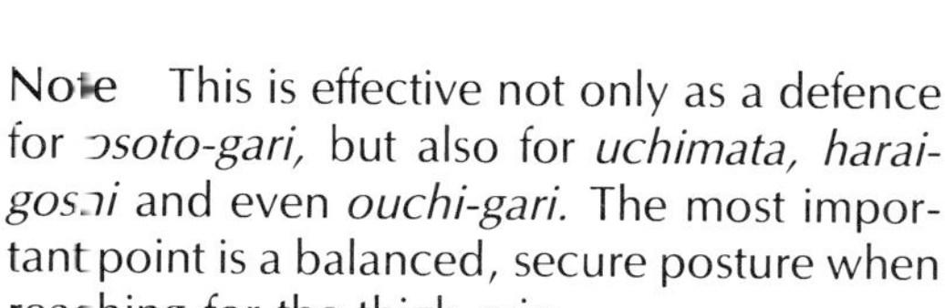

Note This is effective not only as a defence for *osoto-gari,* but also for *uchimata, harai-gosai* and even *ouchi-gari.* The most important point is a balanced, secure posture when reaching for the thigh grip.

At the top level of competition, fighters do not separate these two actions, but turn the whole motion into a timing movement. As the attacker comes in, the defender does not stop the action like a machine, but only checks it slightly, going with the flow. He allows the leg to come across in order to pick up the thigh more easily, and then just lifts in one smooth motion.

Osoto-Gari Countered by Tani-Otoshi (Fig 26)

Keynote

This was my answer when I was attacked by an opponent using *osoto-gari,* but who was right handed – the *kenka-yotsu* situation. It is not impossible to do this against someone with the same-sided grip, but it is harder because the turning action has to be directed by the sleeve grip which is technically quite difficult. So it is best when a right-hander faces a left-hander.

Normally, the first – and the simplest – defence against a *kenka-yotsu osoto-gari* attack is to turn away from it, breaking the opponent's grip on the sleeve. Because of the distance he has to cover, he needs that sleeve grip to pull his opponent across and get in for the throw. When the sleeve grip is not broken, the situation is quite dangerous, especially if he has dominated the other grip, perhaps with a strong high collar grip. An alternative is *tani-otoshi.*

Note   When I was a teenager, I found that I was quite weak when attacked by a right-handed opponent who had taken a high grip with a strong *osoto-gari* or even *uchimata* or *harai-goshi,* and I needed to come up with a solution. The problem occupied me for some time, but when I was in the Japanese national training camp in 1977, I came up with an answer and I threw both Chonuske Takagi and Sumio Endo with this *tani-otoshi* counter. When I met them later in competition, they did not even try to take the high grip and did not attack me with *osoto-gari* or *uchimata.* I was able to win.

(a) My opponent starts to attack.

(b) and (c) I halt the attack, bringing my left hip into play. This is an important movement.

(d) At this point, I release the grip with my left hand, and put my arm around my opponent's waist, drawing him in to me. My weight, of course, must be lower than his. Note the level of our belts in Fig 26(c) and (d).

(e) I do not want simply to fall back in a rather ungainly crunching *tani-otoshi*. Having achieved control of his body, I give him a little push forwards, bringing his weight on his right foot. He is expecting a direct pull back and not a sudden forward movement, so it comes as quite a surprise. However, he feels fairly safe, so he is happy to go with the movement, and makes a small step on his right foot.

(f) With his weight now forward and his body bent, his natural movement pattern brings his left foot off the ground, and he comes forward slightly. This is exactly what I want. My left leg stretches to make contact, and I sweep — hopefully with a smooth, well-timed action.

(g) I do not try to lift at all, just go straight down to the mat, relying on the sweeping action for impetus. I will not get an ippon for this, but possibly a *yuko* or a *waza-ari*.

(h) I need to be really fast into *newaza* to make sure of the ippon in the end. In fact, although I am underneath to start with, it is not difficult to get into a good position for *newaza*, because my opponent will still be a little confused by what has happened. His head often snaps back to indicate this.

(i) I go straight into *yoko-shiho-gatame*.

Osoto-Gari Countered by Nidan-Kosoto-Gari (Fig 27)

Keynote

Another elegant counter against a poor *osoto-gari* attack.

(a) Uke attacks with *osoto-gari,* but there is no break of balance and plenty of space between the two fighters. Already tori has started to defend by pushing against uke's sleeve grip.

(b) Tori pushes harder and starts to turn round.

Note   It is also possible to use this as a combination, although it can be a little risky. Tori attacks with what feels like a poor *osoto-gari.* His opponent twists to counter with *osoto-gaeshi* 1, and then tori counters with *nidan-kosoto-gari.* Perhaps for randori only!

(c) Suddenly — and it must feel like an explosion (which is why the picture is a little blurred! — tori attacks with *nidan kosoto-gari,* aiming for uke's left leg.

(d) The throw is often an indisputable ippon, although *osaekomi* is also virtually inevitable.

Osoto-Gaeshi 1 (Fig 28)

Keynote

This is the traditional counter to *osoto-gari* — *osoto-gari* itself!

(a) and (b) Uke attempts an *osoto-gari,* but he has not broken tori's balance and has no control of tori's head and upper body. He is in a very unstable position.

(c) Tori takes a small step backwards with his left foot, twisting his body, but ensuring that he takes his opponent's upper body with him.

(d) The twisting action is continued during the actual throw.

Osoto-Gaeshi 2 (Major Outer Reap Counter) (Fig 29)

Keynote

This spectacular technique has been used as a counter against *osoto-gari* for many years in Japan, but it has been brought into prominence especially by Russian fighters, with the characteristic lifting knee action. It requires a strong back and leg muscles, but it is a marvellously dynamic action. It can only be used in a *kenka-yotsu* (opposing grips) situation.

(a) and (b) My first important defence is to turn my body away from the *osoto-gari* attack, but I put my weight all on my right foot.

(c) My opponent is not aware of the danger, because I allow him to keep on coming. He feels confident that the attack is still on, especially as he curves his foot around to hook in. It is important to keep some space between the two bodies. If contact is made, my opponent can regain control and throw me.

(d) I have set a trap which now comes into operation. My right knee starts to lift him off the ground.

(e) and (f) He is taken up in the air and I flatten him out with my hands. When I start to put him down, I glance to my left.

(g) I place him down directly in front of me, laying him at right angles to my stance.

Timing

This is not just the power lift it may first appear. While it is an athletic action, it is also very much a timing technique, as this rear view shows.

My opponent is moving forwards, and I capitalise on that movement, going with him.

The feeling of the lift is one of scooping my opponent off the ground in a clean action, not jacking him up. It is useful to practise it with an exaggerated, even bouncy action to get the rhythmic flow.

(h) This is my lifting position.

Taishi – Ambition

Training for Osoto-Gari

Osoto-gari is a good technique to teach to beginners. It involves all the basic elements of judo, *kuzushi,* timing and good balance, and ends with a satisfying thump. It is a throw which can be used at all levels, but whether it is learned at the start of a judo career or later on, the principles are the same.

It is important not to restrict the action, especially at the beginning. It may look like a controlled throw – and it is – but when executed properly, the attacker is able to put every ounce of mental and physical effort into it as well as a certain amount of abandon.

This makes for exciting stuff, but the fundamentals must be drilled in at the start so that when total commitment is called for, the throwing action is not hampered by incorrect details. This is true of most big throws in judo, of course, but especially of *osoto-gari* even though it does not have a big turning action like *uchimata* or *seoi-nage.*

The Learning Process

I learned my judo moves in four different ways:

1. From a teacher. Generally the first and the most common source of knowledge. My teachers introduced techniques to me, made corrections as I worked on them and helped me hone them into useful judo tools.
2. From watching others. I always kept my eyes and ears open everywhere I went (and I still do). If I saw something in a randori or in a competition which interested me, I would note it down and have a look at it later to see if I could put it to good use.
3. Solving a problem. Sometimes, I was faced with a difficulty. I turned it over in my mind, sometimes for weeks on end, and finally came up with a solution. It may have needed some adjustment as time went on, but it provided an answer. My *tani-otoshi* counter to *osoto-gari* from a right-handed fighter was just such an example.
4. Remembering the good times. On occasion something can happen in randori or competition, quite out of the blue. I can be practising with someone much stronger than me, who is throwing me time and again, or I can feel as if I am hitting a brick wall when, suddenly, I find my opponent on his back in front of me.

The temptation is to say to myself: 'That was lucky,' and enjoy the afterglow, but what I should do is file the details away in my brain for future consideration. I should write down what happened as soon as possible so that I can remember it, look at it, check it over and try it again. Obviously, something happened that was absolutely correct. It may have been the *kuzushi* or the timing. It may have been a combination or a reaction. It is too precious to be lost in a moment's jubilation. This is how I discovered my *ouchi-uchimata* combination which made such an impact on my international career. These moments are like gold dust in judo. Remember them.

The Reaping Leg (Fig 30)

Keynote

A considerable amount of solo work (we call it *hitori uchikomi* in Japan) is done by all exponents of reaping throws in order to develop a powerful reaping action. It is not enough just to peck at an opponent's leg. This solo work also strengthens the supporting leg, and ensures that it can bend comfortably and smoothly.

(a) and (b) Supporting myself against a wall, I step forward to simulate the attacking motion of *osoto-gari.* I must imagine my opponent in front of me.

(c) and (d) I step through, going past my imaginary opponent, swinging the reaping leg high. Of course, in competition or randori it never goes as high as this, but by extending the action in *hitori uchikomi* I can develop power for the shorter attacking action.

(e) This stage is not what is generally expected. I do not simply reap high, bringing my head down to the ground in a pivot motion – this is really too easy, and comes naturally in other stages of the preparation work – instead, I take my reaping leg back and down, sinking my weight but maintaining a good posture. This is a much more powerful action, and after thirty a day, strong muscles and a smooth action are developed.

Uchikomi

This is the backbone of the training process for any judo throw. By constant repetition, the body learns the basic movement of the throw.

In order for the movement to become second nature, hours of *uchikomi* are required. Nevertheless, it is important to maintain a lively attention to the details. At the start of the learning process, the *uchikomi* pace enables one to methodically go through a check-list, ensuring that the entry, or the *kuzushi*, or even the reaping action is correct. However tempting, *uchikomi* should not be done mechanically.

Later on, when the main feel for the throw has been acquired, *uchikomi* may take on another meaning, more as part of the warming up process, getting the body working smoothly again after the distractions of the day.

It comes back into its own, however, as a learning process, on the occasions when the technique starts to slip away for some reason which is not apparent. There have been times when I have realised that I am not throwing well with *osoto-gari*, either in randori or competition, and I return to my *uchikomi*, going through the details like a pilot running through the check-list on his plane before taking off. It may be that the fault is in the entry or the *kuzushi*, or it may be in the timing. I may never find it, but, having been back to the basic and having examined my technique, the throw starts working again.

Moving Uchikomi (Fig 31)

(a) and (b) I start off fairly slowly, concentrating on fluid action. I do not want to introduce any jerky movements at all. I ask my partner to step back, but once into my stride, I tend to control our movement, working my arms well.

(c) and (d) These photographs give an idea of the speed I try to maintain once I have got going. I cannot keep it up for long — I can only do around five sets in Tokai Dojo before coming to the end of the mats and turning around, but that is probably about right.

Keynote

The length of my dojo in Tokai University is 20 tatami (around 35m). One of my favourite practices is to cover the whole length practising this form of moving *uchikomi*. I am looking for a relatively light action, with the emphasis on speed. My *tachiwaza* is based on movement and speed — who said that heavyweights cannot move fast? — and this moving *uchikomi* is my workshop.

(e) and (f) As I come level with my partner, I swing my reaping leg high to bring power into the movement, but I do not reap. I just swing my leg down in between my partner and myself the way it came, and start again.

(g) and (h) With a strong push, the sequence is repeated.

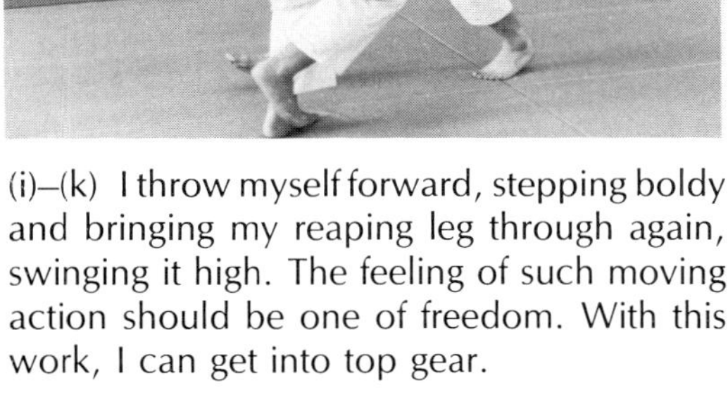

(i)–(k) I throw myself forward, stepping boldy and bringing my reaping leg through again, swinging it high. The feeling of such moving action should be one of freedom. With this work, I can get into top gear.

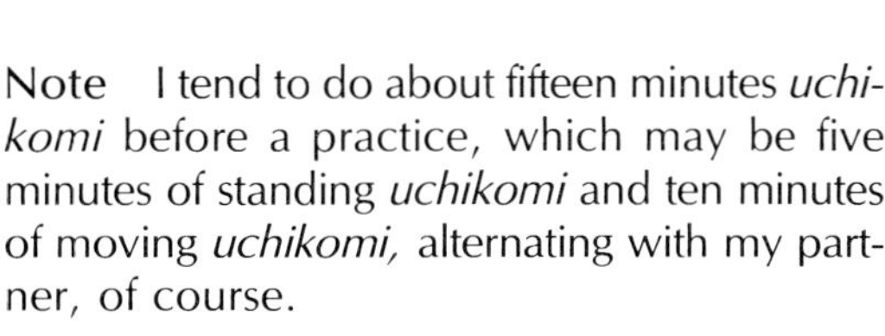

Note   I tend to do about fifteen minutes *uchikomi* before a practice, which may be five minutes of standing *uchikomi* and ten minutes of moving *uchikomi,* alternating with my partner, of course.

Three-Person Uchikomi (Fig 32)

Keynote

This is another favourite *uchikomi* practice, perhaps my most favourite. It is a very different kind of training to the moving *uchikomi*. It is fundamentally a training practice for the reaping leg, and I enjoy it because it requires 100 per cent commitment. It takes a little while for all three people to understand their roles sufficiently to make the most of the practice.

The third man has to keep his position. He must not pull or push, but stay rigid. He stands slightly to one side. The second man has to place all his weight on his left leg (for a left-handed player like me). He must try and keep as upright as he can, making me work all the harder. The attacker reaps with 100 per cent effort. This is an ideal way to develop a very strong reaping action, and also a strong but resilient supporting leg. I step into position, reap and then continue to inject as much effort into the reap as I can for an extra three or four seconds. It is too easy just to come in, reap and come out. In contest, it will often be necessary to give that extra 5 per cent to send your opponent crashing to the mat. Those three or four seconds develop that extra 5 per cent.

Frequency

I do this in various patterns. I can do three or five entries and then one reap (this is quite common in Japan), or I can reap each time I make an entry, but reap with just 70 – 80 per cent power. Finally, I can do one entry, reap 100 per cent and then break. After a moment, I will do it again, 100 per cent, and break. I used to do this before a competition, because it is a good mental and physical exercise.

(a) and (b) I pull myself in, making as great an effort as I can.

(c) and (d) My reaping leg is working lower now, as it would in competition. I reap as hard as I can, and the effect is to nearly take my second man uke over. (The *kuzushi* and the reap have bent him over despite the support of the third man.)

(a) Jean-Michel Berthet (France) shows a classical posture in his osoto-gari at the Tournoi de Paris 1989.

(b) But the completion of the throw reveals a mixed grip – a typical contest manoeuvre.

79

Tōshi – Fighting will

Self-Defence

In the context of judo for self-defence *osoto-gari* is one of the most appropriate of throws for study. Many police forces and military groups employ variants of the throw in their close-quarter combat training. Its popularity can perhaps be explained by the facts that it is relatively easy to perform, does not involve turning the back to the enemy and untrained individuals (non-judoka or those without wrestling experience) are very susceptible to it. This weakness is partly a result of people having very little recovery when thrown to the rear and being unable to see where or how they are going to fall. Often, the person being thrown will focus his attention on the first thing he becomes aware of in the process of the attack: the thrower's hands. These tend to grip high which completely distracts him from the subsequent reaping action of the leg which comes in low and from behind! Adding to this the fact that the fall can be extremely heavy, and where hard unyielding surfaces such as concrete are concerned, potentially fatal, the suitability of the technique for combat becomes apparent.

Osoto-gari has to be practised with care. Trained, experienced judoka have been known to be winded by *osoto-gari* attacks, even on the relatively soft judo mat, despite knowing how to fall correctly. Fighters have, on occasion, been knocked out in contest when they have landed on the back of their heads, such is the impetus of the throw. In the Tournoi de Paris, in 1989, the final of the 65kg category was decided in spectacular and dramatic fashion in only eleven seconds with an *osoto-gari* by the East German Kendalbacher on his French opponent, Hamid Abdoune. The throw was so powerful that the Frenchman was thrown on the back of his head and his body jack-knifed, so that his knees and the back of his head were touching the mat simultaneously. The hapless Abdoune's neck was severely strained and he had to be taken to hospital immediately. On concrete such a throw would undoubtedly have been fatal.

In training for self-defence the emphasis should be on speed and accuracy, rather than power. The technique works on the non-judoka because of its suddenness and unpredictability and these are the factors that ought to be stressed and developed by training.

Osoto-gari is one of the major high-scoring techniques in competition, although this is often because of skilful use of *osoto-gaeshi,* when one fighter uses *osoto-gari* to counter-throw another. Making a half-hearted or weak *osoto-gari* attack is an open invitation to be thrown with an *osoto* counter and cannot be recommended. However, the danger of being countered in this way is not a major factor when considering the application of the technique against an assailant unlikely to be skilled in judo. It remains true to say, though, that you must be fully committed to completing the technique once you decide to use it. The thrower's aim should be to down the opponent as quickly and as suddenly as possible.

There are many possible variations of *osoto-gari* in judo. Usually the relative sizes of the two fighters determines the suitability of a particular type of *osoto-gari,* but real specialists can adapt their basic techniques to cope with any kind of shape or physique. The same is true in self-defence. The truth of the matter is that, in the stress of a self-defence situation, any given individual will do what he has been trained to do. The judoka is likely to employ the technique he feels most confident with, whether it be the most appropriate to the situation or not. Of course, real experts have a wide repertoire of techniques which they are capable of employing should the situation demand it. The less expert are well advised to take stock of their relative strengths and weaknesses and to complement their normal training with specialised self-defence drills, concentrating on what they do well anyway, experimenting with it for self-defence purposes.

One of the great advantages of being an *osoto* specialist when required to use judo in a self-defence situation is the fact that it is one of the throws which is least affected by whether or not your assailant is wearing a jacket. A man wearing a T-shirt can be thrown just as effectively as one in a judogi, simply by gripping the wrist with the left hand and using the right to grip or slap a number of possible targets. The head may be controlled by first slapping and then gripping the face or by placing the heel of the hand under the jaw or even by gripping the throat. Alternatively, the trapezius muscle may be grabbed and the forearm used to control the upper chest. The head is a surprisingly easy structure to grab,

although sport-trained judoka find this a difficult concept to adjust to, as the rules of competition have trained them not to touch the face.

Another major consideration when practising *osoto-gari* in a self-defence context is that of maintaining your balance and not going down with your assailant. If your assailant does decide to grab hold and pull you to the floor with him, the best thing is probably to really up-end him and attempt to fall on top of him and wind him.

The severity of the fall in an application of *osoto-gari* for self-defence purposes makes it most appropriate as a technique to be used against an armed attack where the assailant clearly has serious intentions to damage his intended victim. The following techniques have to be practised assiduously to develop the necessary timing and co-ordination to be effective. Any Dan grade with an acceptable *osoto-gari* will have more than enough power to throw a non-judo-trained assailant, but the essence of effective self-defence lies in good speed of reaction based on the confidence to move unhesitatingly. Here are two examples of *osoto-gari* used in self-defence — against and punch, and a blunt implement (a bottle).

Defence Against a Punch (Fig 33)

Keynote

This is the most common use of *osoto-gari* in a self-defence situation and is of real practical worth. The important principle is to keep the movements direct and simple.

(a) The attacker prepares for a punch attack — it is generally clear from which side the main threat is going to come.

(b) Tori blocks the attack with his forearm and takes his fingers around the arm or elbow for control. He steps into position virtually simultaneously.

(c) Now comes the particular variation suitable for street situations. Tori puts the heel of his palm under the attacker's chin and drives the head backwards none too gently.

(d) Hooking the attacker's right leg in traditional *osoto-gari* fashion, he can feel his opponent way off-balance.

(e) It is simple to drive the opponent onto his back with appropriate force. On a pavement, most attackers will be winded at least.

Defence Against an Assailant Armed with a Bottle (Fig 34)

This is a useful technique to practise as it can be used, unaltered, against virtually any kind of clubbing attack.

(a) The assailant pulls back his right arm to launch a clubbing attack to the head of his intended victim with a wine bottle.

(b) The defender immediately blocks the attack with the outside of his forearm against his assailant's hand. It is not effective or safe to block his forearm because the wrist can bend over the blocking arm and the weapon may still connect with the target. Note how the defender bends the knees to absorb the impact and to position himself to spring into the counter-attack.

(c) The defender grabs his assailant's shirt at the collar bone and immediately counter-attacks.

(d) He swings his right leg through and around behind his opponent, striking his calf into the back of his knee, forcing the leg to bend. He simultaneously drives the arm holding the bottle down to his assailant's side, forcing him off-balance to the rear.

(e) By bending at the waist and sweeping up with the right leg as he pulls down with both hands, the defender can throw his assailant heavily on his back, then, if he remains conscious, disarm him.

Tōkon – Fighting spirit

Competition Osoto-Gari

Of all the major throwing techniques in judo, *osoto-gari* is perhaps the most powerful to perform and certainly one of the most stunning to watch. This is one reason why it has always been one of the top three or four throws in almost every major event, international or domestic, throughout the countries of the world.

The list of tournaments won by *osoto-gari,* and by its proponents are seemingly endless. Furthermore, they are also distinguished by the enormous variety of sizes and shapes of those who have used the techniques. Nakatani is best remembered as having won the final of the lightweight category at the 1964 Olympic Games with footsweeps, but is should not be forgotten that he had a most effective *osoto-gari* which he put to good use in the earlier rounds. And a range of other light-class fighters have made their mark with the throw.

Of course, the powerful nature of *osoto-gari* has made it more the preserve of the heavier weight categories. These range from Peter Seisenbacher, Austria's double Olympic champion at u86kg to the true heavyweights such as Sergei Novikov (Soviet Union), Hitoshi Saito (Japan), Kazuhiro Ninomiya (Japan), Angelo Parisi (France), Wilhelm Ruska and many others.

In Japan it may even be more popular than in the West. Of the seven team members at the 1988 World Championships, four – Naoya Ogawa, Hitoshi Sugai, Testuo Mochida and Shinobu Osako – all counted *osoto-gari* as one of their major techniques.

However, as with many of the main judo throwing techniques, it appears to have become more difficult to bring off *osoto-gari* in its classical form at the very top level of competition. This is partly because the stances can be so defensive and partly because the grips can be so obstructive.

This acute defence can also make *osoto-gari* a dangerous technique to attempt. Once the attack is launched and the attacking leg has hooked across, tori can be extremely vulnerable to a counter if uke's balance has not been broken correctly. To be in that outstretched position, standing on one leg, is not very secure! Perhaps as a result of this, the *osoto-gari* most commonly seen in competition nowadays look like much more of a hook, hop and reap pattern, though the eye does not always tell the full story.

Peter Seisenbacher was generally taller than his opponents and used his long legs to good advantage, although this was something learned from experience. In his early competition career he was countered on a number of occasions after hooking rather casually. He learned that it was vital to hook but keep the reaping pressure on the back of the opponent's calf as he hopped round into a better position to finish the throw. But despite his height, speed and power, very rarely did he manage to move into the ideal reaping position at the start. Frequently, his initial step with his right leg (Seisenbacher attacked left) was made slightly wide, and, once he hooked, he would turn into the throw and reap. Of course, the throw would not have been possible without the strong arm control, drawing the opponent off-balance.

Hitoshi Saito was not born with the long, slim legs of Seisenbacher and had to make the most of his suppleness and good technical control. In the final of the open category of the World Championships in Moscow, in 1983, he faced the much taller Vladimir Kocman

(Czechoslavakia), and *osoto-gari* was not the obvious throw to attempt.

Saito's first movement was to hook. Saito's formidable calf and foot clamped on the back of Kocman's knee and calf and, even though the Japanese champion was actually standing in front of Kocman (and, therefore, in a technically dangerous position for such a manoeuvre), he had compensated by a truly magnificent bash on the nose (purists must read 'break of balance' here) with his collar grip hand. Rocking Kocman momentarily, like an experienced woodsman deciding in which direction to fell a huge tree, he put in an extra hop to get into reaping position, and put the Czech down smack on his back. Once again, it appeared like a hook, hop and reap, but the leverage pressure between the work of the hands and the work of the reaping foot was in play from the moment Saito's foot had connected with Kocman's calf.

When Novikov threw Gunther Neureuter (West Germany) in the final of the open category of the 1976 Olympics in Montreal, it was a thundering *osoto-gari*. But even though Novikov was quite a bit heavier and more powerful than Neureuter, he had to have two goes at it. He stepped in, in a fairly orthodox manner, but Neureuter, being very much aware of the Russian's favourite technique, was ready for it. He began to step off the reaping leg, but he was not prepared for the powerful follow-on action of Novikov who maintained control with his hands and simply lunged forward with his body, so that Neureuter, caught on one heel with one leg high in the air, had nowhere to go but down.

There will always be examples of judo fighters, like Parisi, who by their special flair and explosive speed, or ingrained technical skill, will produce the perfect *osoto-gari* from the initial entry at top competition, though they may be relatively rare. Some may be able to make this *osoto-gari* work at national level only, and will have to adapt it for international level. The best *osoto-gari* specialist will adapt well to the prevailing conditions.

There will always be those who use less elegant versions, and *osoto-gari* comes from a flurry of attacks but there are many other kinds one fighter will take the belt and produce a result, or another will drive into the mat for a *maki-komi*, another last-resort variation. However, *osoto-gari* will remain one of the most important of judo throws in competition as well as in the clubs.

(a) A superb osoto-makikomi *from the 1973 World Championships in Lausanne.*

(a) and (b) The youthful Peter Seisenbacher (Austria) only manages a yuko from this osoto-gari at the 1982 European Championships in Rostock, East Germany; as the opponent manages to turn out.

(a) Alexander Iastkevich, the Soviet middleweight, fought commandingly in the 1980 European Championships. Here, he hooks in with his right leg for the first stage of the attack.

(b) Just how well he has caught his opponent off-balance can be seen by the middle stage where Iastkevich has driven off the back leg and is taking his opponent down to the ground for ippon.

(a)–(c) In the Tournoi de Paris in 1979, I used the same technique of dropping to my knee to bring down my much larger opponent, Alexander Tiurin (Soviet Union) with osoto-gari.

(a) Osoto-gari *attack and defence in the match between Ann Hughes (Britain) (right) and Jenny Gal (Holland) (left) at the 1988 European Championships in Pamplona, Spain.*

(a) The start of one of the finest osoto-gari throws ever photographed. Angelo Parisi was on his way to a massive defeat at the hands of the Russian Olympic champion, Shota Chochosvilli, in the light-heavyweight category of the European Championships. Parisi, fighting for France, had been thrown for waza-ari and three kokas, with just one minute twenty-four seconds remaining. Suddenly, he exploded into the attack, catching the Russian with all his weight firmly planted on one foot.

(b) As he got into position, Parisi started driving for the mat with total commitment of his own bodyweight and impetus.

(c) Instinctively feeling the need for a change of direction, he drew Chochosvilli off to one side, enabling him to take the Russian clean off both feet.

(d) With a roar of triumph, he put the Olympic champion flat on the mat.

(a) and (b) The dangers of osoto-gari. *Neil Adams (Britain) reaches out for a hooking type of* osoto, *but fails to control the opponent's head. His opponent is free to turn into the throw and lifts Adams into the air. In this case, Adams retained sufficient control to extricate himself from the situation without conceding a score.*

Hitoshi Saito (Japan) throws Vladimir Kochman (Czech) with osoto-gari *aided by a useful bash on the nose, in the 1983 World Championships.*

(a) Kisaburo Watanabe was one of the leading Japanese stylists of the 1950s and 1960s, and beat a number of larger yet better-known fighters such as Kaminaga. Matsushita and Koga before forsaking his contest career to come to London to teach at The Budokwai. In one competition in Japan, he produced this text-book osoto-gari.

(a) and (b) At 1979 Tournoi de Paris, I attacked with osoto-gari *and went straight into* kesa-gatame *for ippon.*

(a) A dynamic attacking pattern from the 1984 Tournoi de Paris. The attacker gets into position for osoto-otoshi. Notice that his gripping is quite loose – his left hand has not grasped the collar yet.

(b) Now he has gripped strongly and started to drive off his right foot.

(c) He helps the throwing action by twisting slightly to his right, pulling on both the sleeve grip and the collar grip. This brings his opponent right off the ground.

(d) Notice the angle at which the opponent lands – almost at right angles to the original angle of attack

94

(a) Bashir Varaev (Soviet Union) did, however, manage to bring off the technique in the World Championships, in Belgrade, in 1989, even against an elusive player like Jason Morris (USA). Varaev gets into position with an osoto-gari action, and tries to force the technique from that position.

(b) When it does not work, he switches to a reaping action and it was this that took the American down to the ground for a koka, and decided the contest.

(a) One of the great exponents of osoto-gari, Sergei Novikov (Soviet Union), here throwing Britain's Mark Chittenden at the 1980 European Championships.

Index